SINGLE IN THE CITY

The Single Mom's Ultimate
Guide to Entrepreneurship

Terra Jackson

TABLE OF CONTENTS

INTRODUCTION 1

CHAPTER ONE
YOUR BUSINESS IDEA 5

CHAPTER TWO
FUNDING 10

CHAPTER THREE
COMBINING YOUR RELATIONSHIP WITH
BUSINESS 15

CHAPTER FOUR
HAVE A POSITIVE MINDSET 20

CHAPTER FIVE
BUILDING THE BUSINESS 25

CONCLUSION 29

INTRODUCTION

There is no doubt that we all must have come across the phrase "single mom" at one time or the other. A number of years back, being a single mom was something which was believed to be peculiar to only poor women and minorities. It was usually assumed that only a few number of women who could not fend for themselves could fall into such a category. However, in our society today, single motherhood is something that has now become very common and could even be regarded as a "norm" so to speak. Why is this so? Well, a major factor is the presence of children born outside wedlock which was not so common some decades ago. Did you know that at least 4 out of every 10 children are born to mothers who are not married? Another statistic shows that close to 2/3 of them were born by mothers who had not reached the age of 30. Records are also available to show that about 17.2 million children under the age of 18 are born without a father to raise them. Needless to say, when situations such as these come up, someone has to take care of these children and it is usually up to their mothers to do so singlehandedly.

If you happen to be one of these strong women who have been saddled with the huge responsibility of looking after and nurturing their child or children as the case may be right from birth, I say a big "Well done!" to you. No matter how the issue may be addressed, the truth is that raising kids especially when there is no man around to assist is a very arduous task. However, this job needs to be done and you have proven to be that strong and independent woman by stepping up to do it. That singular action is worthy of praise and commendation. Normally, when the father of a child is not in the picture, it would be expected that he would begin to chip in money for child support which will be used to lookafter the child and take care of his or her needs. However, records show that as much as 62% of single moms get absolutely nothing for child support. Using this statistic, it would mean that in a country where there are about 200,000 single moms, as much as 124,000 out of them receive no money for child support from their children's fathers. How then can you as a single mom take care of yourself and your children as well?

Children require a lot of money in order to take care of them in the best way you can- when you think of their schooling, clothing, feeding, toys and so on, you could become downcast when you begin to realize how much money is needed to take care of all these. If you have a job, it is unlikely that your earnings will be able to cater for you and your child or children effectively. The situation could be even more knotty if you are a single mom who does not have a job at the moment- you might constantly begin to wonder how you can provide for yourself and child since there is now no father around to provide the basic necessities. Do not despair however for all hope is not lost. Up until now, you might never have considered starting up your own business and even if you have, it is possible that you might never have really worked towards making it a reality. The time has now come for you to begin your own business and make it as successful as possible. This book will enlighten you about all you need to know in order to have your own successful business even as a single mom.

CHAPTER ONE
YOUR BUSINESS IDEA

The first step to be taken when starting your own business is to come up with a great business idea. In our society today, so many kinds of businesses can be found and they range from bakeries, salons, stores to gift shops, flower shops and so on. You too can begin your own business today and watch it grow from grass to grace as long as you put in the right amount of effort and have the right attitude. When coming up with an idea for your business, you should endeavor to focus on something relatively new or unusual. This helps to draw attention to your business as potential customers will likely be more drawn to new concepts rather than something common. Try to be original and create something iconic. Explore uncharted waters and when you finally start your business, you'll see that a lot of people will have their interests piqued by your new idea.

As much as it is important to be original when you are coming up with a new idea, it is also equally vital that you focus on working on an aspect which appeals to you. Working on something which you enjoy has an added advantage of making you even more dedicated to the business. When your heart is in something, working on it will be so easy for you and you'll be constantly motivated to do even more and progress to the next level. For example, if you are someone whose favorite thing to do in the world is to bake, you would agree with me that if you have a bakery business, it would be an absolute delight for you to bake cakes for your customers on a daily basis. Having a business which involves something you are fond of makes it even easier for you to work on it and put a great deal of effort into making it successful.

With the situation of things, it is very unlikely that you have a huge amount of money stashed in a vault somewhere. How then can you start up your own business when you have barely enough to live on? You could start by putting 10% of your income away as savings- you can do this by making an allotment to yourself which gets withdrawn as soon as money is available in your account. That way, the allotment will still be made even if you forget and as time goes by, you won't even miss it. You could also cultivate the habit of leaving your credit cards at home. This way, you won't be able to carry cash with you and that helps you to spend wisely and guard against impulsive buying. As much as capital could be a determining factor, you should never let it stop you from achieving your goal. At such a stage in which you are, it is highly recommended that you work on starting a business which requires little or no capital. You do not have enough cash to be channeling so much into a business and so limit the amount of money you make use of in the business. I mentioned that you can opt for a business which needs absolutely no capital- how is this even possible? That is one of the benefits of working on something that you have a passion. For example, if you love baking, it is very likely that you already have all the necessary tools which are needed to start up a baking business. You could make use of your kitchen oven in baking the pastries and voila, your business is up and running. Apart from this, taking up a job as an online writer is also a business that needs no capital- all you need is your computer! Businesses such as these are good options for you as a single mom who is trying to make ends meet.

Lastly, in having a great business idea, it is important that you are as realistic as possible. You are obviously starting with the little amount of resources you can gather and so having your head stuck in the clouds will be of no advantage to you. Set goals that you know you can achieve and when you have achieved the, set even bigger ones and go for them. However, your goals should consist of things that you actually have the ability to do. For example, setting a goal of owning a firm with about 14 offices all over the world after two weeks of starting your business can rightly be classified as building castles in the air. Instead of setting unrealistic goals like this, set more achievable goals such as getting at least one customer every week, designing a website for your business, talking to five people each week about your business and so on. These kinds of goals help to keep you on your toes and constantly motivate you to work even harder thereby improving your business greatly.

Now that you have had an understanding of how you can come up with a great business idea for your start-up, let us now consider 15 vital ways through which you can run a successful business as a single mom in the following chapters.

CHAPTER TWO

FUNDING

Do not let funding discourage you from having the kind of business you want- so many single moms find themselves struggling with funds to take care of their kids and taking care of their home in general. When you think about feeding, clothing, paying fees and getting one or two playthings for your children, what is left is barely enough for you to take care of your business. In situations like these, even the bravest of women could find themselves giving up hope and changing their minds about starting their businesses. If you happen to be one of such women, you should aspire not to give up. Rather, why not think about ways by which you can generate funding for your business? Taking your lunch to work is also very helpful in helping you save money. Spending $8.00

daily on lunch might not seem like a huge amount but multiply that by 22 days and you get about $176 dollars every month.

Another way by which you could save up money for your business is by buying clothes for the next season. This is because clothes are much cheaper in seasons when they aren't worn e.g. buying a winter coat during summer. If you are a mom who likes to go out, make sure you plan for the outing adequately. You could do this by putting your wine or liquor in a flask and then calling it a day rather than buying $10 drinks which are usually watered down. Family and friends could also help you in raising the needed fund for your business. Also, there is a huge number of financial channels which have been put in place specifically for single moms just like you in order to boost their businesses. A good example of such an initiative is the CDFI which is sponsored by the US government. Exploring such channels could help you to get that needed help for your business.

- **Start small-** The importance of this phrase cannot be over-emphasized when it comes to nurturing your own business. No matter the kind of business idea you have, it is necessary that you start with the little resources available to you. Take a cue from my experience and begin to work on improving your business as soon as you have a business idea, a little amount of money to fund it and the right attitude. Even if you are still working towards developing a great business idea, remember that consistency is very important. You can set aside two hours to work on your business ideas daily and then increase it gradually while ensuring that the time set does not interfere with the time you have to hang out with your kids.

- **Create goals for yourself and your life-** Apart from helping to motivate you, goals also help you to have a mental picture of the exact thing you are working towards. For example, if you set a goal of setting up a website for your online store in a period of two weeks, you know what it is you are aiming for and the necessary steps to be taken. Asides work or business goals, you should also set life goals for yourself- you might wonder why this is important. Well, life goals help to give your life a meaning. When you set out to do something and you are able to achieve it, it gives you a sense of fulfillment and this in turn spurs you on to set even bigger goals and then strive to achieve them. When you are setting goals, you should make sure that you set goals that take you out of your comfort zone. This way, you are able to improve yourself and test new grounds while working on the things that matter in your life. Also, you should keep your goals updated from time to time as this will help you to have things to aspire to constantly.

- **Take good care of yourself-** The popular idea of what a single mom looks like is someone who is haggard, stressed out and have barely enough to live on. This notion is present in the minds of so many people out there and you should never let it get to you. Instead of getting weighed down by such thoughts, you should do all you can to make yourself look perfect. Remember that having the right mental attitude is key to being able to achieve all that you want to achieve. If you are already defeated in your mind and believe that every negative thing that someone says about your situation is true, then it will be quite difficult for you to prove them wrong. Work out every day and try to visit people whose company you enjoy on a weekly basis. Laugh as much as you can. Indulge in volunteer works and abilities which give you fulfillment and happiness. Partaking in things such as these will eventually help in making you a better person and that way you have even more to give to your children.

CHAPTER THREE

COMBINING YOUR RELATIONSHIP WITH BUSINESS

Stay away from jerks- Now, there is no doubt that the person you date will definitely have an effect on you and your business as well. Therefore, it is very important that whoever will have that great opportunity of dating you should have all it takes to keep you- he should serve as a motivator, guardianand helper when it comes to your passions and business. Any kind of man who feels that your own success or big dreams is a threat to him should be avoided by all means. One other characteristic of a man who would be a hindering to you and your business is someone who would rather keep you all for himself rather than give you the needed time and support to work on your business and take care of your kids. He will have a hard time giving you the freedom to work on your owndreams while he has absolutely no dream or goal for himself. You should make a mental note to yourself that you should never date any kind of man who makes it difficult for you to reach your goals and boost your business. Be assured that the right man who will be able to keep you will come along in due time.

Request for help when you need it- As a single parent with a budding business, there is no doubt that you will have so many things to attend to and this could weigh you down greatly. Therefore, it is necessary that you get help to avoid getting overwhelmed by the pressure of it all. It could be quite hard to get a nanny who would care for your kid or kids on a full-time basis but do not despair, there are so many other ways by which you can get that extra help and you do not necessarily need to break a bank for you to get access to them. One single mom relates that when she was starting her own business, she hired college students to help her with her kids and her business as well. While they were helping her with business projects and proposals, she had time to look after her kids and spend quality time with them and the times when she needed to work on her business by herself, these students would help her with her kids and also take care of certain things in the home. As a single mom, you could also take this kind of step thereby boosting your business while ensuring that your kids get all the attention they need.

Involve your kids in your business- No matter the type of business you run, it is necessary that your kids are also carried along. Your family has to be a part of your business for it to truly be successful. See your kids as your board of directors who you have to report everything that goes on in your business to. Let them be part of that journey and as we all know that children learn better through the things they see and do, you will also be teaching your kids how to be great entrepreneurs just like you in the future. Of course, you do not want to weigh your kids down with more tasks than they can possibly handle and so you should give them just the kinds of tasks that will not be too much work for them. For example, you can give them tasks like getting the mail, picking up litter and disposing of them properly, stapling some papers and so on. Asides for such activities, you could also join forces with them in coming up with something creative for your business such as deciding on a name for it or picking out colors for the business.

Have a budget for yourself- It could rightly be said that one of the most difficult parts of being a single mom is the financial aspect. When you consider the fact that about 62% of single moms do not get any child support, then you would understand why money is usually hard to come by. This statistic would also explain why a lot of single moms usually dive into the world of entrepreneurship- so as to make ends meet and to better their financial statuses. That being said, one way by which you can have a hold on your finances is by having a realistic budget for yourself. Have a great plan for those days when your business might not move properly as it normally would. With this, you'll be able to save for the rainy day and also make sure that such times do not have a negative effect on your business. Apart from having a budget for your business, you also need to budget for your household. As mentioned earlier, money is not a commodity that is usually in surplus in a house where only one parent is present. Therefore, you should have a budget which will guide you when it comes to purchasing certain things. When you stick to this budget, you can then make use of any excess money to improve your business and move it forward.

CHAPTER FOUR

HAVE A POSITIVE MINDSET

Be proud of your situation- A major ingredient in having a successful business is confidence and when this important ingredient is absent, your customers or potential customers are able to detect it. You have to own your status as a single mom and rock it well. It all begins with the right attitude and you need to understand that being a single mom is not a disability which you need to be ashamed of or hide. The fact which a lot of people do not realize is that being a single mom equips you even better to be able to have a successful business. How is this so? Well, you have already been exposed to all the characteristics which are essential in the workplace and they include the ability to multitask, manage, operate on a budget, delegate, solve problems and so on. With these features coming to play on a daily basis in your home, there is no doubt that you have all the essentials needed to run a successful business. With that being said, you should never allow anyone to make you feel threatened or incapable simply because of your situation. You should always wear the single mom medal proudly on your neck wherever you may find yourself.

Strike a balance between your life and your work- There is something known as the "work-life balance" and what it simply entails is balancing both your work and your life so that none of them gets neglected. As a single mom, striking this balance between your life and your work might not be as easy as it sounds and this is why a whole lot of single moms have refrained from setting up their own businesses. It cannot be argued that being a mom requires a lot on the part of the mother but at the same time, it can equally be said to be very rewarding. As demanding as it could be, being able to balance it all will make it possible for you to handle it. Needless to say, there will be times when your business will require more attention than your kids and there will be times when you will need to give more attention to your children over your business. You just have to ensure that your children really understand what is going on and do not feel neglected. When you make sure of this, it will be possible for you to achieve that desired balance you need between your work and your life.

Eliminate all negative influences- to begin with, what is or who is a toxic influence? To put it in clear terms, toxic influences are people who constantly tell you that you are a single parent and that the major thing you should be focusing on is taking care of your kids without actually telling you how to take care of them. They are those people who never give out compliments or words of encouragement but keep on telling you that growing a business is hard and that you will never be able to build anything. You should realize that you do not need such negativity in your life and should get as far away from it as you can. Having anything to do with people who constantly point out the problems your business has without actually stating the way forward is detrimental to your business's healthas they are sure to dampen your spirit and bring you down in the long run. As it is, you barely have enough time to cater for your children and also keep an eye on your business. Therefore, you should cut of all ties with pessimistic people who constantly invade your confidence and make it harder for you to make progress.

Organize your life and business- In a typical single mom's home, there is usually a whole lot of activities going on talk less of a single mom is owns a business also. Engaging in a conference call while also preparing your kids for school could be quite a battle which requires a lot of strength and courage. However, it is possible for you to get your act together without losing a limb. The secret is to come up with fireproof organizational systems for your life and your business too. Thanks to technology, there are a whole lot of apps available for free on the internet which you can make use of in order to keep your life organized and detailed. An example of such apps is Hootsuite which helps you in tracking and managing all the social network channels which you might have. Apart from these apps, you could also make use of to-do lists and reminders on your phone to help you have a hold on things. If you are not a big fan of using smartphones and all of the applications that can be gotten on it, you could resort to the usual low-tech methods which you are very familiar with. An example of such methods is the common sticky notes which can be gotten at a local store. As usual as they might seem, these can be used to achieve a level of orderliness in your life. For example, you could simply write down a list of the things which you want to achieve in a week and then stick it on your worktable, fridge or any place where you are sure to see it. This way, you are constantly reminded of the things which you have plans to achieve.

CHAPTER FIVE

BUILDING THE BUSINESS

Flexibility is important- A major thing that is constant in life is change and it applies to everyone including single moms. To be a successful single parent, it is necessary for you to be adaptable to all kinds of situations. You need to learn how to make the best use of whatever resource is available to you while remaining optimistic and proactive at the same time. Juggling all of your activities and adjusting to each situation in which you find yourself is important if you really want to have a successful business. As I mentioned earlier, change is constant in life and as a result of this, your children will surely grow, your business will definitely evolve and even you will experience some changes. Of course, you would agree that the attention a toddler would require would not be the same with that which a child of 8 years would need. In your business also, when you begin to broaden your reach and work towards getting more customers, it would be necessary for you to pay even more attention and devote more time to your business. Knowing that various stages of your life will require different versions of you should motivate you to be even more flexible and open to new methods.

Tap into the experience reserve of other people- When it comes to growing your own business, the truth is that the best way for you to get the needed knowledge is by making use of the wisdom of other people who have already walked down that road successfully. It does not matter where you get such knowledge from- whether from books, websites, networking groups, seminars and so on, you should always seek out knowledge from different people. This is important because they have already gone through the kinds of experience which you are likely to come across and now know the best way by which such things can be taken care of or avoided as the need may be. They have the "do's and don'ts" about business and tapping into their "experience reserve" will help you to know the actions which you need to take so as to boost your business and those which you should avoid at all costs. No doubt, "experience is the best teacher" but even if you have not gone through that particular experience yourself, you can learn from the experiences of other people and then use it to the best of your advantage.

Create time- Regardless of what you are working on at moment, you should never neglect spending quality time with your children. Although it could be tempting to postpone hanging out with your children, it is important that you consider them with every move you make in your business. If you discover that a particular business idea which you have might take up all of your time leaving you with no time for your kids, you might need to scrutinize your plans once again and adjust it in a way by which your children will not be terribly affected. There should always be time for you to take a walk in the park with your kids, attending a school event with them, going out to see a movie and so on. Times such as these help to strengthen the bond between you and your children and it also serves as an avenue for you to take a break from the stress of work and simply enjoy being with your kids. That is one great advantage of being a business owner- you are able to make certain changes and tweaks to your schedule in order to accommodate important issues that could come up and there is no doubt that spending time with your children is pretty important.

CONCLUSION

We have now come to the end of this book. Hopefully, it has been able to affect your life in so many beautiful ways. As mentioned in this book, being a mom is not an easy task; that task becomes even harder when there is nobody to support you or serve as a helping hand. Regardless of that, you need to allow three major things to keep spurring you on towards achieving your goals. The first thing is your child or children who are depending on you for survival and who are learning from your actions or inactions- if you decide to give up on your goals, be sure that they are watching and if you do all you can to achieve them and make them a reality, be rest assured that they are paying maximum attention also. Whatever step you take, remember that your child or children is\are taking a cue from the way you handle the situation. Another motivating factor should be your longing to show the world how awesome you truly are. When you work hard to show the world that you have the ability to overcome every challenge you may come across, you are letting everyone know how much of a strong and independent woman you are. You should have a really strong will to thrive and survive against all odds and situations in which you find yourself. The final factor that should keep you working towards your goals is no one else but you. A favorite saying of mine concerning life and its many ups and downs is "Everything you've ever needed lies within you; tune out and tune in". This simply means that you never have to seek anything outside yourself- no matter what happens in your life, you have all that you need.

Work very hard to use your present situation to your advantage; use it to better yourself and you will be able to have the satisfaction that comes with knowing that there is no obstacle that you cannot overcome and no mountain that you cannot climb.

www.ingramcontent.com/pod-product-compliance
Lightning Source LLC
Chambersburg PA
CBHW031516210526
45464CB00007B/2932